# First World War
## and Army of Occupation
# War Diary
## France, Belgium and Germany

9 DIVISION
1 Lowland Brigades
Highland Light Infantry
15th (Service) Battalion (1st Glasgow).
1 April 1919 - 31 October 1919

WO95/1776/2

The Naval & Military Press Ltd
www.nmarchive.com
**Published in association with The National Archives**

Published by

## The Naval & Military Press Ltd

Unit 10 Ridgewood Industrial Park,

Uckfield, East Sussex,

TN22 5QE England

Tel: +44 (0) 1825 749494

www.naval-military-press.com

www.nmarchive.com

*This diary has been reprinted in facsimile from the original. Any imperfections are inevitably reproduced and the quality may fall short of modern type and cartographic standards.*

© **Crown Copyright**
**Images reproduced by permission of The National Archives, London, England, 2015.**

# Contents

| Document type | Place/Title | Date From | Date To |
|---|---|---|---|
| Heading | Lowland Late 9 Division 1 Lowland Brigade 15th H.L.I 1919 Apr-1919 Oct | | |
| War Diary | Solingen Germany | 01/04/1919 | 30/04/1919 |
| Heading | War Diary of 15th Battalion Highland Light Infantry For Month Ending 31st May 1919 | | |
| War Diary | Solingen Germany | 01/05/1919 | 18/06/1919 |
| War Diary | Grafrath Germany | 19/06/1919 | 30/06/1919 |
| Heading | War Diary of 15th Bn Highland Light Infantry 1st August To 31st August 1919 | | |
| War Diary | Dormagen Germany | 01/08/1919 | 14/10/1919 |
| War Diary | Duren | 15/10/1919 | 28/10/1919 |
| War Diary | Duren Germany | 29/10/1919 | 31/10/1919 |

LOWLAND LATE 9 DIVISION

1 LOWLAND BRIGADE

15th H L I
1919 APR — 1919 OCT

(From 32 DIV 14 BDE)

Form 1480S 77344   15 H61   Army Form C. 2118.

# WAR DIARY
## or
## INTELLIGENCE SUMMARY.
*(Erase heading not required.)*

41.0
10 sheet

| Place | Date | Hour | Summary of Events and Information | Remarks and references to Appendices |
|---|---|---|---|---|
| Solingen Germany | 1919 March 1 | | A & B Companies training under own arrangements. C & D Companies carried on Manning of Outpost Line | 7.1 |
| | 2 | | A & B Companies training under own arrangements. C & D Companies carried on Manning of Outpost line. C Coy captured 1 Officer and 20 men for work on rifle range. Lieut. M. V. R. Barton reverted to duty. Battle on attended service on the North of the French Area | 7.1 |
| | 3 | | C & B Companies training under Company arrangements. C & D Companies carried on Manning of Outpost line. Battalion attended "Brigade Polveren" Reversal on "The Barlow Tangle" | 7.1 |
| | 4 | | A & B Companies training under own arrangements. C & D Coo carried on Manning of Outpost Line | 7.1 |
| | 5 | | Current Rict-vindecation for Commanding Officer. Battalion Sports Commenced. Lieut. Col. F. M. Murray from 2/5 M.C.B. assumed command of the Battalion vice Lieut. Col. V. R. Amoster 9/5 M.C. | 2/5 MC 7.1 |
| | 6 | | Church Parades held in Church Voluntary service in Evening | 7.1 |

# WAR DIARY
## or
## INTELLIGENCE SUMMARY.
(Erase heading not required.)

Army Form C. 2118.

| Place | Date | Hour | Summary of Events and Information | Remarks and references to Appendices |
|---|---|---|---|---|
| Windsor Barracks | 7 | | Training under Company arrangements. C Coy supplied Officers and 20 Men for work on rifle range | TM |
| | 8 | | Training under Company arrangements. Companies bathed | TM |
| | | | Training under Company arrangements. Signallers training under Signalling Sergeant 'A' McCormick out for duty | TM |
| | 9 | | Battalion Route March. Signallers training under Signalling Sergeant. | TM |
| | 10 | | Companies training under own arrangements | TM |
| | 11 | | A.B.& C. Coo of 52nd H.L.I. amalgamated with same Cos of 15th H.L.I. Party of 20 C. Coy men working on rifle range. C and B. Coo | TM |
| | 12 | | attended lecture in Barracks at 17.30 hours. Morning spent re-organising. Appts inspected by Commanding Officer. | TM |
| | 13 | | Church Parade as usual. | TM |
| | 14 | | Training under Coy arrangements. 40 Men at Work on Rifle Range. B & C. Cos bathed. A & B. Coo. C. Webb inspected by Co. Commanding. TM. Football match 52nd H.L.I. v. 15th H.L.I. result 3-2 in 52's favour. | TM |

Army Form C. 2118.

# WAR DIARY
## or
## INTELLIGENCE SUMMARY.
(Erase heading not required.)

Instructions regarding War Diaries and Intelligence Summaries are contained in F. S. Regs., Part II. and the Staff Manual respectively. Title pages will be prepared in manuscript.

| Place | Date | Hour | Summary of Events and Information | Remarks and references to Appendices |
|---|---|---|---|---|
| Johnson Germany | 15 | | Company training. A. Coy. supplies 20 men for work on range. B. Coy. bathed in public baths. Lieuts Robertson, Keith and Barr proceeded for demobilisation. | TPP |
| | 16 | | Parades under Coy arrangements. 20 men supplied for work on rifle range. | TPP |
| | 17 | | Training under Coy arrangements. Lieut McCormick and Lieuts Blair and Park proceeded to demobilisation. | TPP |
| | 18 | | Divine Services in Church. Lieuts Traces & Smith proceeded for demobilisation. | TPP |
| | 19 | | A and B Coys training under Coy arrangements. B Echelon and kits of B. & C. Coos inspected by Commanding Officer. Capt. R.S. Chalmers and Lieut R.A. Tait proceeded for demobilisation. | TPP |
| | 20 | | Church Services. Voluntary service in evening. Lieuts J.R. McGregor, L.G. Shaw, R.S. Gross, R. Eaton, R.P. Smith and Lieuts L.C. Duff and A.D. Smith proceeded for demobilisation. | TPP |

# WAR DIARY
## or
## INTELLIGENCE SUMMARY.
*(Erase heading not required.)*

Army Form C. 2118.

| Place | Date | Hour | Summary of Events and Information | Remarks and references to Appendices |
|---|---|---|---|---|
| Solumbes | 21 | | Holiday. Band & D Coy bathed | TM |
| Germany | 22 | | Company training. Headquarters Coy. Transport and Stores bathed. | TM |
| | 23 | | B & C Coy training under Coy. arrangements. A & D Coy. bathed | TM |
| | 24 | | Ceremonial Parade. 20 men at work on rifle range. Company training. C & B Coy bathed. Lecture in Recreation "The Policy of Germany since 1864" attended by B & D Coys. | TM |
| | 25 | | B Co training. B Co Headqrs at Ceremonial Parade. C Co. & A Co training. 21 men at work on rifle range. D Co. at Baths | TM |
| | 26 | | Company training. Commanding Officer inspected Billets. Football match 51st H.L.I. v. 15/4/21. 15th London 7 to 1. M.O.S.O. Game abandoned. Lieut-Col H.M. Craigie-Halket assumed command of the Battalion vice Lieut Col J.M. Murray, vice J.S.O. M.C. | TM |
| | 27 | | Church Parades as usual. Voluntary Communion Service in evening | TM |

Army Form C. 2118.

# WAR DIARY
## or
## INTELLIGENCE SUMMARY.
*(Erase heading not required.)*

Instructions regarding War Diaries and Intelligence Summaries are contained in F.S. Regs., Part II. and the Staff Manual respectively. Title pages will be prepared in manuscript.

| Place | Date | Hour | Summary of Events and Information | Remarks and references to Appendices |
|---|---|---|---|---|
| Solingen Germany | 1919 April 28 | | Training under Company arrangements. Officer and 20 men at Rifle Range. Battalion bathed. | 7A |
| | 29. | | A. and D. Coy. Ceremonial Parade. B & C Coy. training. B, C & D Coy. attended under Company arrangements. | 7A |
| | 30 | | Lecture on Laboratory by Rev. Canon Heywood. Companies training under own arrangements. | 7A |

| | 1st April | | 30 April | |
|---|---|---|---|---|
| | O.R.S. | O.R. | O.R.S. | O.R. |
| Commanding Officers Strength | 22 | 551 | 26 | 1082 |
| Fighting Strength | | | | |
| Officers | 34 | | 49 | |
| Other Ranks | 718 | | 1466 | |

Wm Coughlin Lieut Lt. Col.
Commanding 5 Bn Highrs L.I.

# WAR DIARY
## or
## INTELLIGENCE SUMMARY.
(Erase heading not required.)

Army Form C. 2118.

Instructions regarding War Diaries and Intelligence Summaries are contained in F.S. Regs., Part II. and the Staff Manual respectively. Title pages will be prepared in manuscript.

| Place | Date | Hour | Summary of Events and Information | Remarks and references to Appendices |
|---|---|---|---|---|
| Shapur | April | | C & B Companies training under own arrangements. | 781 |
| | | | C & B Companies carried on Wiring of Outpost Line | |
| January | 2 | | A & B Companies training under own arrangements. C & B Companies | 781 |
| | | | carried on wiring of Outpost Line. C Coy supplied 1 Officer and 20 | |
| | | | men for work on rifle range. 2/Lieut M.H.B Bolton joined for duty. | |
| | | | Battalion attended lecture on "The Work of the French Army in English" | 781 |
| | 3 | | A & B Companies training under Company arrangements. C & D Companies | 781 |
| | | | carried on Wiring of Outpost line. Battalion attended Lecture in | |
| | | | Kaiserani on "the Burma Jungle". | 781 |
| | 4 | | A & B Companies training under own arrangements. C & D Coy | 781 |
| | | | carried on Wiring of Outpost line | |
| | 5 | | Conducted Billet inspection by Commanding Officer. | 781 |
| | | | Battalion Sports Comm'ee formed. Lieut Col J.M. Murray, 1st Yorks L.I | |
| | | | assumed command of the Battalion vice Lieut-Col W.B Amesden DSO MC. | 781 |
| | 6 | | Church Parades held in Church. Voluntary service | 781 |
| | | | in evening | |

# WAR DIARY
## or
## INTELLIGENCE SUMMARY.

Army Form C. 2118.

(Erase heading not required.)

| Place | Date | Hour | Summary of Events and Information | Remarks and references to Appendices |
|---|---|---|---|---|
| Achiet-? | April | | | |
| Germany | 7 | | Training under Company arrangements. C Coy supplied 1 Officer cent 20 men for work on rifle range | |
| | 8 | | Training under Company arrangements. C Company bathed under Signalling Sergeant Lieut J. M. McCormick went on duty | |
| | 9 | | Battalion Route March. Signallers training under Signalling Sergeant | |
| | 10 | | Company's training under usual arrangements. A, B & C Coys of 52nd H.L.I. amalgamated with same Coys of 4/5th H.L.I. | |
| | 11 | | A, B & C Coys of 52nd H.L.I. amalgamated with same Coys of 4/5th H.L.I. Camp B Coy. party of 30 C Coy men working on rifle range. attended Lecture on Discipline at 17.30 hours | |
| | 12 | | Morning spent re-organising Billets to inspected by Commanding Officer. | |
| | 13 | | Church paraded as usual. | |
| | 14 | | Training under Coy arrangements. 40 men at work on Rifle Range. Bn. C Coy bathed. A & D Coy billets inspected by Commanding Officer. Football match 52nd H.L.I. v. 15th H.L. I. result 3-2 for 52nd | |

**WAR DIARY**
or
**INTELLIGENCE SUMMARY.**

Army Form C. 2118.

| Place | Date | Hour | Summary of Events and Information | Remarks and references to Appendices |
|---|---|---|---|---|
| Solesmes Germany | 15 | | Company training. A Coy supplied 20 men to work pigeon range & B Coy bathed in public baths. Lieuts Robertson, Keith and Kerr proceeded for demobilisation. | |
| | 16 | | Parades under Coy arrangements. 20 men supplied for work on rifle range. | |
| | 17 | | Training under Coy arrangements. Lieut McCormick and 2nd Lieuts Prow, Cock, McEwen, Laub and Park proceeded for demobilisation. | |
| | 18 | | Divine services in Church. Lieut's Gairdner Smith proceeded for demobilisation. | |
| | 19 | | A and D Coys training under Coy arrangements. Billet and kits of B & C Coo. inspected by Commanding Officer. Capt. N. B. Chalmers and Lieut N. G. A. Tait proceeded for demobilisation. | |
| | 20 | | Church services. Voluntary service in evening. Lieuts R. McGregor, L.G. Shaw, N.S. Grass, W.R. Bacon, R.P. Smith and Lieuts L.C. Duff and A.H. Smith proceeded for demobilisation. | |

Army Form C. 2118.

# WAR DIARY
## or
## INTELLIGENCE SUMMARY.
(Erase heading not required.)

Instructions regarding War Diaries and Intelligence Summaries are contained in F. S. Regs., Part II. and the Staff Manual respectively. Title pages will be prepared in manuscript.

| Place | Date | Hour | Summary of Events and Information | Remarks and references to Appendices |
|---|---|---|---|---|
| Solingen Germany | 21 | | Holiday. Band & D Coy. bathed. | 751 |
| | 22 | | Company training. Headquarters Coy. Transport and stores bathed. | 751 |
| | 23 | | B & C Coy. training under Coy. arrangements. A & D Coy. | 751 |
| | 24 | | Ceremonial Parade. 20 men at work on Rifle Range. Company training. C & B. Coy bathed. Lecture in Kaserned "The Ruler of Germany since 1864" attended by B & C Coys. | 751 |
| | 25 | | A Coy. training. B Coy troops at Ceremonial Parade. 9 Coy at Barks. 21 men at work on rifle range. | 751 |
| | 26 | | Company training. Commanding Officer inspected Battn. Football match 5/1st H.L.I. v 15/H.L.I. 15th leading 7 to 1. Game abandoned. Lieut-Col. H.M. Craigie-Halkett resumed Command of the Battalion vice Lieut. Col. D.H. Murray Lyon D.S.O. M.C. | 751 |
| | 27 | | Church Parades as usual. Voluntary Communion Service in evening. | 751 |

Army Form C. 2118.

# WAR DIARY
## or
## INTELLIGENCE SUMMARY.
(Erase heading not required.)

Instructions regarding War Diaries and Intelligence Summaries are contained in F. S. Regs., Part II. and the Staff Manual respectively. Title pages will be prepared in manuscript.

| Place | Date | Hour | Summary of Events and Information | Remarks and references to Appendices |
|---|---|---|---|---|
| Solingen Germany | April 28 | | Training under Company arrangements. 1 Officer and 20 men at Rifle Range. Battalion bathed. | A/1 |
| | 29 | | Class B "C" Company Parade 8 to 6 hrs training under Company arrangements. B & D Coys attended Lecture on Rehearsal by Divisional Magnate. | A/1 |
| | 30 | | Companies training under Coy arrangements. | A/1 |

| | 1st April | | 30 April | |
|---|---|---|---|---|
| | OFF. | O.R. | OFF. | O.R. |
| Commanding Officers since 1916 | | | 26 | 1088 |
| Fighting Strength | | | | |
| Officers | 34 | | 49 | |
| Other Ranks | | 718 | | 1466. |

A.M. Craig Helm ??
Lieut. Col.
Commanding 15th Batt Highrd Lght Infy

WAR DIARY

OF

15th BATTALION HIGHLAND LIGHT INFANTRY

FOR MONTH ENDING 31st MAY, 1919.

Army Form C. 2118.

# WAR DIARY
## or
## INTELLIGENCE SUMMARY.
*(Erase heading not required.)*

Instructions regarding War Diaries and Intelligence Summaries are contained in F. S. Regs., Part II. and the Staff Manual respectively. Title pages will be prepared in manuscript.

| Place | Date | Hour | Summary of Events and Information | Remarks and references to Appendices |
|---|---|---|---|---|
| Solingen Germany | May 1 | | Fine - Warm - Battalion Route March - Solingen - Wald - Gräfrath - Solingen | Ap. |
| | 2 | | Fine - Warm - C.O. Billet and kit inspection | Ap. |
| | 3 | | Very Warm - School parade as usual | Ap. |
| | 4 | | Warm - Battalion Ceremonial Parade. Preparation for inspection | Ap. |
| | 5 | | Very Hot - Parade same as previous day | Ap. |
| | 6 | | Fine - Warm - Battalion is conveyed in 30 Buses to Leverkusen for inspection by H.R.H. the Duke of Connaught, Colonel-in-Chief of the Highland Light Infantry. During his inspection H.R.H. made favourable comments on the appearance and steadiness of the men. In the afternoon H.R.H. passed through Solingen in his car, and was enthusiastically cheered by the troops at various points. | Ap. |
| | 7 | | Very Warm - Coy. Training & Recreational Training resumed | Ap. |
| | 8 | | Fine - Warm - Battalion Route March - Solingen - Wald - Shys - Solingen | Ap. |
| | 9 | | Very Hot - Working Party on range Stokeberg. Parade minus Coy. arrangements | Ap. |

# WAR DIARY
## or
## INTELLIGENCE SUMMARY.
*(Erase heading not required.)*

Army Form C. 2118.

| Place | Date | Hour | Summary of Events and Information | Remarks and references to Appendices |
|---|---|---|---|---|
| Solingen Germany | MAY 10 | | Lovely day - Rather hot - C.Os Billet inspection. Football Inter- Bgde. Inter-Coy Competition "B" Coy 15 H.L.I. v "D" Coy 51st A.L.I. Hard game | Am |
| | 11 | | Quiet 51st H.L.I. 15th H.L.I. 0 | |
| | | | Fine - Warm - Church parade as usual | Am |
| | 12 | | Dull - Warm - R.S.M's Parade. Training as per programme. Working party on Range Stokenberg | Am |
| | 13 | | Clear Hot - Training as per programme. Working party on Range Stokenberg. Lecture by Archdeacon Jones on "British Character Building" | Am |
| | 14 | | Very warm - Battalion Ceremonial Drill Working party on Range | Am |
| | 15 | | Very warm - Training as per programme - Lt-Col H.M Grange-Hallett CMG, DSO proceeded on leave to U.K. Lt-Col A.B.Thorburn assumes Command during absence on leave of Lt-Col Grange-Hallett CMG DSO - Working party on Range Stokenberg. Lecture People of the Orient - Middx Bellingham | Am |
| | 16 | | Dull - Hot - Training under Coy arrangements. Working party on Range | Am |
| | 17 | | Warm - Dry - C.Os Billet inspection. Lecture "The Fallacy of Bolshevism" by Lt. Col. Thorburn. Transfers 150 O.Rs to 51st H.L.I. 14 O.Rs to 6th Bn D.L.I. Route March by Coy | Am |

2.8th Fd. Amb. 4.8 O.Rs 35 O.Rs

Army Form C. 2118.

# WAR DIARY
## or
## INTELLIGENCE SUMMARY.
*(Erase heading not required.)*

Instructions regarding War Diaries and Intelligence Summaries are contained in F. S. Regs., Part II. and the Staff Manual respectively. Title pages will be prepared in manuscript.

| Place | Date | Hour | Summary of Events and Information | Remarks and references to Appendices |
|---|---|---|---|---|
| Schuinies Hoogte Germany | MAY 18 | | Fine - Hot - Church Parade as usual | A1 |
| | 19 | | Day - Very Warm - Training under Coy arrangements | A2 |
| | 20 | | Dull - H.L. - Training under Coy arrangements. Working party on Range (Sunday) | A3 |
| | 21 | | Very Warm - Road March Cancelled - Training under Coy arrangements | A4 |
| | 22 | | Fine - Warm - Training under Coy arrangements. Working party on Range Shooting | A5 |
| | 23 | | Troops Church parade 8.30 a.m. Usual Training under Coy arrangements | A6 |
| | 24 | | Very Hot - Training under Coy arrangements. Working Party on Range Shoreberg | A7 |
| | 25 | | Warm - Church Parade as usual | A8 |
| | 26 | | Very warm - Training as per Programme. Two hours educational training | A9 |
| | 27 | | Very warm - Training under Coy arrangements | A10 |
| | 28 | | Very warm - Training under Coy arrangements | A11 |

# WAR DIARY
## or
## INTELLIGENCE SUMMARY.
(Erase heading not required.)

Army Form C. 2118.

| Place | Date | Hour | Summary of Events and Information | Remarks and references to Appendices |
|---|---|---|---|---|
| Solingen Germany | 29 | | Very warm - Training under Coy arrangements | An |
| | 30 | | Fine - Warm - Training under Coy arrangements | An |
| | 31 | | Fine - Very Hot - Commanding Officer inspection of Billets & also working party on Range Stockerberg | An |
| | | | | |
| | | | | 1st May | 31st May |
| | | | | Off / O.R.s | Off / O.R.s |
| | | | | 26 / 1050 | 24 / 770 |
| | | | Commanding Strength | | |
| | | | Fighting Strength | | |
| | | | Officers | 35 | 31 |
| | | | Other Ranks | 1306 | 1024 |

O.B. Harcourt Lt. Col
Commanding 15th Bn. Highd L. Infy

Army Form C. 2118.

# WAR DIARY
## or
## INTELLIGENCE SUMMARY.
*(Erase heading not required.)*

Instructions regarding War Diaries and Intelligence Summaries are contained in F. S. Regs., Part II. and the Staff Manual respectively. Title pages will be prepared in manuscript.

| Place | Date | Hour | Summary of Events and Information | Remarks and references to Appendices |
|---|---|---|---|---|
| | | | | |

Army Form C. 2118.

# WAR DIARY
## or
## INTELLIGENCE SUMMARY.
*(Erase heading not required.)*

Instructions regarding War Diaries and Intelligence Summaries are contained in F. S. Regs., Part II. and the Staff Manual respectively. Title pages will be prepared in manuscript.

| Place | Date | Hour | Summary of Events and Information | Remarks and references to Appendices |
|---|---|---|---|---|
| Contich | January 1 | 9a | Troops to be below having water toys arrangements | App |
| | | 9b | Usual G.S. & G.O. inspection of Billets | App |
| | | 2p | M.O. Chiefs Parade as usual | App |
| | | 2p | Warm bath having under Bn arrangements. Battalion Baths on Convent School Street. | App |

| | 1st | 2nd | 3rd | 4th | HQ & Tpt's |
|---|---|---|---|---|---|
| Trench fighting Officers strengths | | | | | |
| Fighting Strengths | 30 | 115 | 31 | 1103 | |
| Officer | | 33 | | 26 | |
| Other Ranks | | 761 | | 811 | |

For G Allen Capt
Commanding 1st/5th E. E. Regt

1st Foss.

H.H.O
3 sheets

War Diary

of

15th Bn. Highland Light Infantry

1st August to 31st August 1919

**Army Form C. 2118.**

# WAR DIARY
## or
## INTELLIGENCE SUMMARY

*(Erase heading not required.)*

**15th Battalion The Highland Light Infantry.**

| Place | Date | Hour | Summary of Events and Information | Remarks and references to Appendices |
|---|---|---|---|---|
| Dormagen, Germany. | Augt. 1st | | Dull and Showery. 'A' and 'B' Coys. training under Coy. arrangements. 'C' and 'D' Coys. on Company Training. 2/Lieut. G.A.Danskin and 2/Lieut. A.Mealor joined the Battalion and were posted to 'D' and 'C' Coys. respectively. | |
| | 2nd | | Dull. Training as Previous day, and C.Os.inspection of Billets. | |
| | 3rd | | Church Parades as usual. 2/Lieuts. Danskin and Mealor joined Battalion | |
| | 4th | | Dull - mHld. Holiday. | |
| | 5th | | Warm. 'A' and 'B' Coys. training under Coy arrangements. 'C' and 'D' on Company Training. | |
| | 6th | | Warm. Training as previous day. Lena Ashwell Concert Party gave entertainment in Dining Hall at night. | |
| | 7th | | Very warm. Training as Tuesday. Lieut. T.D.Murphy assumed command of 'B' Coy. 2/Lieut. R.J. Douglas assumed the duties of Assistant Adjutant. Battalion Dance in Dining Hall at night. | |
| | 8th | | Very warm. Training as previous day. | |
| | 9th | | Very warm. C.Os. Billet and Kit inspection. | |
| | 10th | | Intense Heat. Church Parades as usual. Cricket Match in afternoon Officers v/ Sergts'. Decisive win for Officers. | |
| | 11th | | Intensely hot. Training as Friday. | |
| | 12th | | Very warm. Training as previous day. Lecture by Rev. O.E.R.Wheeler C.F. "The Palestine Campaign." Major R.P.Burnett D.S.O.M.C. South Staffs Regt. joined for duty as second in command. Capt. Buchanan posted from 16th H.L.I. and assumed command of 'B' Coy. | |
| | 13th | | Very warm. Training as Monday. | |
| | 14th | | Very warm. Training as previous day. Battalion Dance in Dining Hall. | |
| | 15th | | Very warm. Training as previous day. | |
| | 16th | | Mild. C.Os. Kit inspection. | |
| | 17th. | | Showery. Church parades as usual. | |
| | 18th. | | Warm. 07.00 - 08.00 Adjutants Parade. 08.00 - 09.00 Under Coy. arrangements. 09.15 - 10.15 Education. | |
| | 19th. | | Training as previous day. Battalion issued with Divisional sign. | |
| | 20th. | | Showery. Training as Tuesday. | |
| | 21st. | | Heavy rain. Training as previous day. | |
| | 22nd. | | Rain. Battalion Route March in Fighting Order. Feet inspection. | |
| | 23rd. | | Rain. C.Os. Billet inspection. 2/Lieut. J.M.Eadie proceeded on leave. Lieut. H.J.Younger transferred to U.K. 2/Lieut. R.J.Douglas proceeded to concentration camp for demob. | |
| | 24th | | Rain. Church parades as usual. | |
| | 25th. | | Warm. Training as previous week. Lecture by Capt. K.H.Seton Kerr on 'Wild Beasts and Men I met in India. Brigade Sports held on Battalion Sports ground in afternoon. Aggregate championship, | |

# WAR DIARY
## or
## INTELLIGENCE SUMMARY

*(Erase heading not required.)*

Army Form C. 2118.

| Place | Date | Hour | Summary of Events and Information | Remarks and references to Appendices |
|---|---|---|---|---|
| DORMAGEN, GERMANY. | Aug. 26th. | | Warm. Training as Monday. Battalion Dance in Dining Hall. | Lt. B. Foster. Capt. 9/9/19 |
| | 27th. | | Cold. Training as previous day. 2/Lieut. R.Macdonald assumed the duties of Assistant Adjt. | |
| | 28th. | | Cold. Battalion on Tactical exercises. Battalion Dance in Dining Hall. | |
| | 29th. | | Cold. 07.00 Adjutant's parade. 08.00 - 09.00 Training under Coy. arrangements. 09.45 - 10.45 Education. Lieut. A.W.Cave rejoined for duty and posted to 'B' Coy. | |
| | 30th. | | Mild. Tactical exercises (Attack on a village). | |
| | 31st. | | Cold. Church parades as usual. | |

|  | Strength at 31/8/19 | | Strength at 31st Aug | |
|---|---|---|---|---|
| | Officers | O.Rs. | Officers | O.Rs. |
| Commanding Officers Strength | 28 | 1002 | 28 | 946 |
| Total | 28 | 1002 | 28 | 946 |

Lt. B. Foster Capt. 9/9/19
for Lieut-Col.
Command. 15' Bn Highl. L.I.

**Army Form C. 2118.**

**WAR DIARY**
or
**INTELLIGENCE SUMMARY**
(Erase heading not required.)

1st Mons
15th Batt. Highland Light Infantry

450
3 sheets

| Place | Date | Hour | Summary of Events and Information | Remarks and references to Appendices |
|---|---|---|---|---|
| Bonnaugh Camp | Feb. 1st | | Dull. cold. Training. - 07.00 - 08.00 Adjutant's Parade. 08.00 - 09.00 under Coy. arrangement. 09.45 - 10.45 Education. | |
| | 2nd | | Warm. Parade as previous day. | |
| | 3rd | | Bright - warm. Tactical exercise - defence of a village. Convoy in Bonnaugh. Running held at night by "Fragments". 10 min Party. babi. 2m. F. O'Malley joined for duty. | |
| | 4th | | Warm - breezy. Training under Coy. arrangements. Examination for 2/c + 3/c class. Certificate held. Battalion Concert Party. "The Hunjos" gave successful concert in Bengal Hall. | |
| | 5th | | Warm. Battalion Route march. Gus inspection | |
| | 6th | | Very warm. Col's Rifles and Kit inspection. Lunch. "Duty" men sent for dinner. | |
| | 7th | | Dull. mild. Church Parade as usual. | |
| | 8th | | Very warm. 07.00 08.00 hr. Adjutant's Parade. 08.00 - 09.00 Training under Coy. arrangements. 09.45 - 10.45 Education. 35 "Duty" men sent for dinner. | |
| | 9th | | Very warm. Training under Coy. arrangement. | |
| | 10th | | Warm. 07.00 - 8.00 Adjutant Parade: 08.00 - 09.00 Musketry. 09.45 - 10.45 Education. | |
| | 11th | | Warm. Battalion Route march. | |
| | 12th | | Mild. Training under Coy. arrangement. | |
| | 13th | | Mild 07.00 - 08.00 Adjutant's Parade; 08.00 09.00 Musketry; 09.45 - 10.45 instruction | |

# WAR DIARY or INTELLIGENCE SUMMARY

Army Form C. 2118.

| Place | Date | Hour | Summary of Events and Information | Remarks and references to Appendices |
|---|---|---|---|---|
| Bermingen Summary | Sept | 14th | Warm. Church Parade as usual. | |
| | | 15th | Very wet. Training under Coy. arrangement. | |
| | | 16th | Dull. Training under Coy. arrangement: 24 men from each Coy. firing on Miniature Range. | |
| | | | 04-30 - 10-00 hour. B.O.s Ceremonial Parade. | |
| | | 17th | Dull. Training as previous day. "B.O's" Dinner Party gave entertainment in Dining Hall. | |
| | | 18th | Dull. Coys. inspection. m.o. and C.O. Parade. | |
| | | 19th | Sunny. Battn. Route march. Dance in Dining Hall at night. | |
| | | 20th | Sunny. 04-00 - 08-30 Musketry - Range. B.O's Billets etc. inspection. | |
| | | 21st | Dull. Church Parade as usual. | |
| | | 22nd | Dull & cold. 04-00 - 08-30 Training under Coy. arrangement. 09-30 - 10-30 Steady Drill. | |
| | | | Officers Ramsay passed from "A" to "B" Coy. Football match. Batt + R.G.2. Win for Batt 4-1. | |
| | | 23rd | Sunny. Training under Coy. arrangement. | |
| | | 24th | Sunny. Training as previous day. Men from 2.Y.m Reserve Battalion. | |
| | | 25th | Sunny. Training as previous day. Dinner in Dining Hall. | |
| | | 26th | Dull-Sunny. 07-00 - 08-00 Musketry Range. 09-30/10-00 hr. Adjutants Ceremonial Parade | |
| | | 27th | Dry wet B.O's Billets < his inspection | |
| | | 28th | Fine & Sunny. Church Parade as usual. | |
| | | 29th | Dull & very cold. Training under Coy. arrangement. | |

# WAR DIARY
## or
## INTELLIGENCE SUMMARY

Army Form C. 2118.

| Place | Date | Hour | Summary of Events and Information | Remarks and references to Appendices |
|---|---|---|---|---|
| Ramage Camp | 1st | 3º | Bright - cold. Training under Coy. arrangement. Lieut A.W.S. Agar M.C. Lecture to all Platoon Commanders, Platoon Sergts. on "musketry": 60 interviewed men who desired information on demobilisation and re-enlistment. | |

Commanding Officers Strength

| | Strength as 31st Aug. | | Strength as 30th Sept. | |
|---|---|---|---|---|
| | Officers | O.Rs. | Officers | O.Rs. |
| | 10 | 1038 | 10 | 188 |
| | 28 | 946 | 29 | 188 |
| | 28 | 946 | 29 | 188 |
| Total | | | | |

Ino. B. Fulton, Capt — 1/4
for Lieut.-Col.
Comdg. 1/5th Hyd. L.I.

**WAR DIARY or INTELLIGENCE SUMMARY**

Army Form C. 2118.

| Place | Date | Hour | Summary of Events and Information | Remarks and references to Appendices |
|---|---|---|---|---|
| Germany Germany | 10th | 1st 2nd | Dull cold. Training under Bn. arrangements. 1655. Whist Drive in Dining Hall, now B Coy NCOs mess — Bn. Training as Previous day. Football match in afternoon Officers v. Sergts. Officers defeated 5 goals to 1. | Letter Cattrall |
| | | 3rd | Showery. 08.45 – 09.45 Education: 10.30 – 11.00. B.Os. Inspection and Ceremonial Parade. No joint Concert Party gave successful entertainment in Dining Hall. Football match in afternoon B.Cay v C Coy in Saturday Battalion League. D Coy's win for C Coy 3-0. | |
| | | 4th | Dull, cloudy. Training under Coy. arrangements. 1900. Rifles & Kit inspection. | |
| | | 5th | Bright and cold. Church Parade as usual. | |
| | | 6th | Cold, misty. Training — Education, P + B.I. Coy Drill & Marching of Arms. Musketry. 1655. Whist Drive in Battalion Dining Hall. Football match "D" v "B" Won for "B" 3-1. "A" Coy v "C" Won for "C" Bn. | |
| | | 7th | Dull & colder. Training as previous day. Football match A Coy v C Coy. Won for C Coy. 10th. Jt Logan lectured to convalescing camps for officers. | |
| | | 8th | Bright, cold. Training as Wednesday. Football match in afternoon — Officers v Sergts. Sergts. Won 1-0. | |
| | | 9th | Cold. Training as previous day. 2nd half match — Pres. v R.O.T. Won for Pres. 2-1. Dance in Bn. Dining Hall at night. | |
| | | 10th | Dull, very cold. Education & Inspection. Pres. twice paraded in afternoon. Gym B.O. Concert Party — Father Sullivan — gave successful service in Dining Hall at night. | |
| | | 11th | Dull & bright. Training under Coy arrangements. 1905. Rifle & Kit inspection. | |

# WAR DIARY or INTELLIGENCE SUMMARY

Army Form C. 2118.

(Erase heading not required.)

| Place | Date | Hour | Summary of Events and Information | Remarks and references to Appendices |
|---|---|---|---|---|
| Dormagen Germany | Oct. | 12th | Showery. Church Parade as usual. | |
| | | 13th | Still & cold. Batn. prepare to move to Düren. Farewell Dance in Dining Hall at night. | |
| | | 14th | Very cold. "A", "C" & "D" Coys move to Junckenburgh Barracks, Düren. "B" Coy. remains at Dormagen to hand over to 4/4th Munst. Division. | |
| Düren | | 15th | Very cold. Day spent in cleaning & arranging Billets. | |
| | | 16th | Very cold. Showery. Cleaning Billets. | |
| | | 17th | Cold. Training under Coy. arrangement. Football match v Royal Scots (1st Bn) Lost - 3-2. | |
| | | 18th | Mild. Training under Coy. arrangement. G.O.C. Billet Kit Inspection. | |
| | | 19th | Very mild. Church Parade as usual. | |
| | | 20th | Mild. Training under Coy. arrangements. Football match 2/6th Roy. Scots Royals R/S. 3. 14.L.I. 2. | |
| | | 21st | Dry - cold. Training as previous day. "B" Coy. returns from Dormagen. | |
| | | 22nd | Frosty. Training as usual. | |
| | | 23rd | Colder. Training under Coy. arrangement. | |
| | | 24th | Mild. Training under Coy. arrangement. Working party from "B" Coy. as Ordnance Dump. | |
| | | 25th | Cold. Coy. Commanding Officer's Billet & Kit Inspection. | |
| | | 26th | Very cold. Church Parade as usual. | |
| | | 27th | Wet & cold. Training under Coy. arrangement. | |
| | | 28th | Dry - cold. Training as previous day. | |

**Army Form C. 2118.**

# WAR DIARY
## or
## INTELLIGENCE SUMMARY
*(Erase heading not required.)*

| Place | Date | Hour | Summary of Events and Information | Remarks and references to Appendices |
|---|---|---|---|---|
| Billet Armory | Oct | 29th | General Training under Coys arrangements. | |
| | | 30th | Church 08:45 - 09:15 Deductions 10:00 - 12:30 Re organisation of Coys. | |
| | | 31st | Wet day. Training as Sunday 30th. | |

Commanding Officer Strength.

| | Strength as at 30th Sept. | | Strength as at 31st Oct. | |
|---|---|---|---|---|
| | Officers | O.R.s | Officers | O.R.s |
| | 29 | 788 | 28 | 622 |
| Totals | 29 | 788 | 28 | 622 |

James B. Ritson
Captain & Adjutant.
for Lieut Colonel.
Commanding 15th Battalion H.L.I.

www.ingramcontent.com/pod-product-compliance
Lightning Source LLC
Chambersburg PA
CBHW081504160426
43193CB00014B/2592